Scottish Rite Handbook

JAMES F. HATCHER III

ISBN-13: 978-1505338638
ISBN-10: 1505338638

Available from Amazon.com, CreateSpace.com,
and other retail outlets

www.CreateSpace.com/5145761

Published by The Masonic Press.
Find more related titles on our website:

masonicpress.com

Printed by CreateSpace, Charleston, SC
An Amazon.com Company

THIS BOOK BELONGS TO

_____
NAME

_____
VALLEY

_____
PHONE

_____
EMAIL

IF FOUND, PLEASE CONTACT THE OWNER AND ARRANGE FOR THE RETURN OF THIS VERY PERSONAL RECORD BOOK.

DEDICATION

This book is dedicated to all of those Freemasons, who, year after year, decade after decade, century after century, have and will continue to strive to help others and work hard to make the world we live in a better place for those of our future generations.

AUTHOR JAMES F. HATCHER III

TABLE OF CONTENTS

ACKNOWLEDGMENTS

Special thanks goes out the Supreme Council, Scottish Rite of Freemasonry, and the Scottish Rite Bodies of North America for selected text, and to Jeff Day at kingsolomonslodge.org for the use of selected Masonic logo graphics.

SCOTTISH RITE
OF
FREEMASONRY

SCOTTISH RITE CREED

Human Progress is our Cause, Liberty of Thought our Supreme Wish, Freedom of Conscience our Mission, and the Guarantee of Equal Rights to All People everywhere our Ultimate Goal.

SCOTTISH RITE MOTTO

Virtus Junxit, Mors Non Separabit

THE DOUBLE-HEADED EAGLE OF LAGASH

Adapted from the
United Supreme Council Website
www.unitedsupremecouncilnjpha.com

The Double Headed Eagle of Lagash is the oldest Royal Crest in the World... No emblematic device of today can boast of such antiquity. Its origin has been traced to the ancient city of Lagash. It was in use a thousand years before the Exodus from Egypt and more than two thousand years before the building of "King Solomon's Temple.

As time rolled on, it passed from the Sumerians to the men of Akkad, from the men of Akkad to the Hittites, from the denizens of Asia Minor to the Seljukian Sultans from whom it was brought by the Crusaders to the Emperors of the East and West, whose successors were the Hapsburgs and the Romanovs.

In recent excavations, the city-emblem of Lagash was disclosed also as a lion headed eagle sinking his claws into the bodies of two lions standing back to back. This is evidently a variant of the other eagle symbol.

The city of Lagash is in Sumer in Southern Babylonia, between the Euphrates and the Tigris and near the modern Shatra in Iraq, Lagash had a calendar of twelve lunar months, a system of weights and measures, a banking and accounting system and was a center of art, literature, military and political power, five thousand years before Christ.

In 102 B.C. the Roman Consul Marius decreed that the Eagle be displayed as a symbol of Imperial Rome. Later, as a world power, Rome used the Double-Headed Eagle, one head facing the East the other facing the West, symbolizing the universality and unity of the Empire. The Emperors of the Holy Roman Empire continued its use and the symbol was adopted later in Germany during the halcyon days of conquest and imperial power.

So far as is known, the Double-Headed Eagle was first used in Freemasonry in 1758 by a Masonic Body in Paris - the Emperors of the East and West. During a brief period the Masonic Emperors of the East and West controlled the advanced degrees then in use and became a precursor of the "Ancient Accepted Scottish Rite."

The Latin caption under the Double-Headed Eagle - "Spes Mea in Deo Est" translated is "My Hope Is In God."

1 SCOTTISH RITE OF FREEMASONRY

Adapted from the Valley of Detroit Website
www.32nddegreemasons.org
and the
United Supreme Council Website
www.unitedsupremecouncilnjpha.com

The Scottish Rite is one of the two branches of Freemasonry in which a Master Mason may proceed after he has completed the three degrees of Symbolic or Blue Lodge Masonry. The other branch is known as the York Rite, consisting of Royal Arch Masons, Royal and Select Masters, and Knights Templar. The Scottish Rite includes the degrees from the 4° to the 32°.

The use of the word "Scottish" has led many Masons to believe that the Rite originated in Scotland. There was also a false belief which persisted for many years, that a man had to go to Scotland to receive the 33°. Neither of these statements is true.

Actually, the first reference to the Rite appears in old French records where the word "Ecossais," meaning Scottish, is found. During the latter part of the 17th Century, when the British Isles were torn by strife, many Scots fled to France and resumed their Masonic interests is that country. It is believed that this influence contributed to the use of the word "Scottish."

In 1732, the first "Ecossais," or Scottish Lodge, was organized in Bordeaux, one of the oldest and most influential Masonic centers in France. The membership included Scottish and English Masons. The years 1738-40 saw the formation of the first "Hauts Grades" or advanced degrees. In 1761, certain Masonic authorities in France granted a patent to Stephen Morin of Bordeaux to carry the advanced degrees across the sea to America. In 1763, Morin established these degrees in the French possessions in the West Indies. What he established consisted of a system of 25 so-called higher degrees which flourished in France, and which were known as the "Rite of Perfection."

Within a few years after 1763, other degrees were added, until the Rite had a ritual structure of 33 degrees — the first three being exemplified in a Symbolic Lodge, if a Grand Lodge with subordinate Lodges existed in the area.

In 1767, Henry Francken, who had been deputized by Morin, organized a Lodge of Perfection in Albany, New York. This was the forerunner of what was to become the Ancient Accepted Scottish Rite in the United States. During the Colonial Period, other deputies, appointed by Morin, organized Masonic groups which conferred the advanced degrees at other important points along the Atlantic seaboard, including Charleston, South Carolina. These groups were independent and without centralized supervision or control; however, they all agreed that their authority came from Stephen Morin in Jamaica in the West Indies.

On May 31, 1801, the Supreme Council of the Thirty-third degree for the United States of America — the first Scottish Rite Supreme Council in the world-was founded in Charleston, South Carolina. Its aim was to unify these competing groups and to bring Masonic order out of chaos. The full membership of this Supreme Council consisted of 11 Grand Inspectors General.

Of these 11 — John Mitchell, Frederick Dalcho, Abraham Alexander, Emanuel De La Motta, Thomas Bartholomew Bowen, Israel De Lieben, Isaac Auld, Le Comte Alexandre Francois Auguste de Grasse, Jean Baptiste Marie Delahogue, Moses Clava Levy and James Moultrie — nine were born abroad and only Brothers Isaac

Auld and James Moultrie were native born. In religion, four were Jews, five were Protestants, and two were Roman Catholics.

On August 5, 1813, Emanuel De La Motta, 33°, of Savannah, Georgia, a distinguished Jewish merchant and philanthropist, and Grand Treasurer General of the Supreme Council at Charleston, organized in New York City the Supreme Council of the Thirty-third degree for the Northern District and Jurisdiction of the United States of America.

The first Sovereign Grand Commander was Ill Daniel D. Tompkins, 33°. He filled this office from 1813-25. He was at the same time Vice President of the United States for two terms, under President Monroe. The first Grand Secretary General of this Supreme Council, its Conservator during the era of anti-Masonic attacks, and its third Sovereign Grand Commander from 1832-51, was Ill John James Joseph Gourgas, 33°.

Both the Northern and the Southern Jurisdictions made slow progress in unifying the scattered degree-conferring groups, and in standardizing the rituals. They were handicapped by the pride in the local organizations; by leadership jealousies; by the anti-Masonic agitation of 1826-40, which almost destroyed Freemasonry; by the War between the States, and by other matters. The process of unification, however, was completed in the Northern Masonic Jurisdiction by the Union of 1867, when the last irregular Supreme Council finally acknowledged the authority of the regular Supreme Council. From that Union, there arose what is the present Supreme Council for the Northern Masonic Jurisdiction of the United States of America.

Since it is now officially recognized as beginning in 1801 in Charleston, South Carolina, the Scottish Rite has spread throughout the world At the present time, the Supreme Council for the Northern Masonic Jurisdiction officially recognizes and enjoys friendly relations with the Supreme Councils of the Scottish Rite in 39 other Jurisdictions, and the higher degree systems (Swedish Rite) administered by the Grand Lodges in the four Scandinavian countries (Denmark, Iceland, Norway and Sweden).

The Northern Masonic Jurisdiction specifically covers the 15 states east of the Mississippi River and north of the Mason-Dixon Line and the Ohio River, including Delaware. Its headquarters is in Lexington, Massachusetts, a suburb of Boston.

The Supreme Council, Southern Jurisdiction, in the United States covers the remaining 35 states, the District of Columbia, and the United States territories and possessions. It has its headquarters at Washington, D.C.

The Northern Masonic Jurisdiction (NMJ) of the Scottish Rite has tinkered with and updated the degrees that Freemason Albert Pike created in the 1860s. The NMJ believes that modern Freemasons get the most impact from the degrees if some of those degrees tell age-old morals and truths by using references more familiar to modern Freemasons.

The 20th degree, Master Ad Vitam, tells a story about George Washington; the 25th degree, Master of Achievement, is about Benjamin Franklin; and the 26th degree, Prince of Mercy, concerns Abraham Lincoln.

The first Scottish Rite organization among African-Americans was the African Grand Council of 1820 in Philadelphia, which was referred to as a Council of Princes of Jerusalem. This Council arose through West Indian migration, for Stephen Morin had propagated the Rite there. The Organization of the King David Supreme Council grew out of the conferring in Philadelphia (1850) of the 33rd Degree by Count DeSaint Laurent (also, Larine) of the Supreme Council of France and the Grand Commander of the Council of Spain on David Leary, the first Black Inspector-General of the Prince Hall Scottish Rite.

In New York City, a Supreme Council of the United States was established in 1864. Also in 1864, a separate Supreme Council was formed in New York, which was made up of members from the National Compact Grand Lodge, from which a Southern Jurisdiction split off with the Headquarters in Baltimore, Maryland. From the Philadelphia Council, a Southern and Western Jurisdiction defected with Headquarters at Washington, D.C. In

1871 a fifth was established in Philadelphia, and was named King Fredrick Supreme Council. In 1881-1887, these five merged into 2 United Supreme Councils of the 33rd Degree: one for Northern Jurisdiction and one for Southern Jurisdiction.

Ill. Edward M. Thomas petitioned the King David Council, since he was residing in the District of Columbia, for the 33rd degree to be conferred on representative Masons in D.C., and on May 5, 1856, the conferment was made and a council was established. A fourth council was set up in Baltimore, Maryland and a fifth Council in Philadelphia. These 5 Councils petitioned for unity in a conference in New York City on January 13, 1881, and was responsible for the Articles of Union and two Supreme Councils of the Northern Jurisdiction (PHA) and the United Supreme Council of the Southern Jurisdiction (PHA).

The constitutions for the Southern Jurisdiction were established in 1887 and revised in 1917 and 1955. The Southern Jurisdiction for the United Supreme Council, PHA, consists of the states: AL, AR, FL, GA, KT, LA, MD, MS, Missouri, NC, OK, SC, TN, TX, VA, WV, the territories of Arizona, New Mexico, the District of Columbia, and Alaska. The Northern Jurisdiction consists of the following states: CO, Connecticut, DE, ID, Illinois, IN, IO, KA, Maine, Mass, MI, Minnesota, Montana, Nebraska, Nevada, NH, NJ, NY, ND, OH, OR, Pennsylvania, RI, SD, UT, VT, Washington, Wisconsin, Wyoming, and that of the states outside Continental United States. Alaska shall belong to the Northern also.

As a result of the conference of the Sovereign Grand Commanders of the two Supreme Councils, Northern and Southern Jurisdictions A.A.S.R., PHA, on August 2, 1966, were established at the Cathedral, Fitzwater & Mole St. in Philadelphia, Pennsylvania. The above divisions were made based on a boundary developed by a joint committee in Wilmington, Delaware on April 19, 1907 using the Mason-Dixon Line as an official boundary.

The Supreme Council is the governing body of the Scottish Rite in the various jurisdictions, and charters all subordinate bodies. Voting members of the Supreme Council are chosen from among those members who have obtained the 33°. These members are referred to as Active Members.

One important point which must be recognized by all Masons is the fact that the Scottish Rite shares the belief of all Masonic organizations that there is no higher degree than that of Master Mason. The Supreme Council and its subordinate bodies acknowledge the Masonic supremacy of the Symbolic Grand Lodges, and the Grand Master of Masons is recognized as the ranking Masonic officer present when in attendance at any Scottish Rite meeting.

Our degrees are in addition to and are in no way "higher" than Blue Lodge degrees. Scottish Rite work amplifies and elaborates on the lessons of the Craft. It should never be forgotten that termination of a member's Symbolic Lodge standing automatically terminates his Scottish Rite membership, whether his rank be 14° or 33°.

Concordant Bodies and Degrees within the Scottish Rite of Freemasonry, Southern Jurisdiction

LODGE OF PERFECTION, 4°-14°
CHAPTER OF ROSE CROIX, 15°-18°
COUNCIL OF KADOSH, 19°- 30°
CONSISTORY, 31°- 32°
COURT OF HONOR
    Knight Commander of the Court of Honour (KCCH)
    Grand Cross of the Court of Honour (GCCH)
SUPREME COUNCIL
    Thirty-Third Degree (33°), Inspector General

DEGREES:

4°   Secret Master
5°   Perfect Master
6°   Intimate Secretary
7°   Provost and Judge
8°   Intendant of the Building

9°   Elu of the Nine
10° Elu of the Fifteen
11° Elu of the Twelve
12° Master Architect
13° Royal Arch of Solomon
14° Perfect Elu
15° Knight of the East, or Sword, or the Eagle
16° Prince of Jerusalem
17° Knight of the East and West
18° Knight Rose Croix
19° Grand Pontiff
20° Master of the Symbolic Lodge
21° Noachite, or Prussian Knight
22° Knight of the Royal Axe, or Prince of Libanus
23° Chief of the Tabernacle
24° Prince of the Tabernacle
25° Knight of the Brazen Serpent
26° Prince of Mercy, or Scottish Trinitarian
27° Knight of the Sun, or Prince Adept
28° Knight Commander of the Temple
29° Scottish Knight of Saint Andrew
30° Knight Kadosh, or Knight of the White and Black Eagle
31° Inspector Inquisitor
32° Master of the Royal Secret, or Knight Commander of the Court of Honour
33° Inspector General

Concordant Bodies and Degrees within the Scottish Rite of Freemasonry, Northern Masonic Jurisdiction

LODGE OF PERFECTION, 4°-14°
COUNCIL OF PRINCES OF JERUSALEM, 15°-16°
CHAPTER OF ROSE CROIX, 17°
COUNCIL OF KADOSH, 18°
CONSISTORY, 19°- 32°
COURT OF HONOR
    Knight Commander of the Court of Honour (KCCH)
    Grand Cross of the Court of Honour (GCCH)

SUPREME COUNCIL
Thirty-Third Degree (33°), Inspector General

DEGREES:

4°   Master Traveler
5°   Perfect Master
6°   Master of the Brazen Serpent
7°   Provost and Judge
8°   Intendant of the Building
9°   Master of the Temple
10° Master Elect
11° Sublime Master Elected
12° Master of Mercy
13° Master of the Ninth Arch
14° Grand Elect Mason
15° Knight of the East
16° Prince of Jerusalem
17° Knight of the East and West
18° Knight of the Rose Croix
19° Grand Pontiff
20° Master ad Vitam
21° Patriarch Noachite
22° Prince of Libanus
23° Knight of Valor
24° Brother of the Forest
25° Master of Achievement
26° Friend and Brother Eternal
27° Knight of Jerusalem
28° Knight of the Sun
29° Knight of St. Andrew
30° Grand Inspector
31° Knight Aspirant
32° Sublime Prince of the Royal Secret
33° Sovereign Grand Inspector General

Concordant Bodies and Degrees within the Ancient and Accepted Scottish Rite of Freemasonry-Prince Hall Affiliation, Northern

Jurisdiction, U.S.A., Inc.

LODGE OF PERFECTION, 4° - 14°
CHAPTER OF ROSE CROIX, 15° - 18°
COUNCIL OF KNIGHTS KADOSH, 19° - 30°
CONSISTORY OF SUBLIME PRINCES OF THE ROYAL SECRET, 31° - 32°
COURT OF HONOR
    Knight Commander of the Court of Honour (KCCH)
    Grand Cross of the Court of Honour (GCCH)
SUPREME COUNCIL, 33°

DEGREES:

4°   Secret Master
5°   Perfect Master
6°   Intimate Secretary
7°   Provost and Judge
8°   Intendant of the Building
9°   Elect of Nine
10° Elect of Fifteen
11° Sublime Elect of Twelve
12° Grand Master Architect
13° Master of the Ninth Arch
14° Grand Elect, Perfect and Sublime Mason
15° Knights of the East or Sword
16° Prince of Jerusalem
17° Knight of the East and West
18° Knights of the Rose Croix
19° Grand Pontiff
20° Grand Master of All Symbolic Lodges or Master ad Vitam
21° Noachite or Prussian Knight
22° Knights of the Royal Axe or Prince of Libanus
23° Chief of the Tabernacle
24° Prince of the Tabernacle
25° Knight of the Brazen Serpent
26° Prince of Mercy
27° Knight Commander of the Temple
28° Knight of the Sun

29° Knights of St. Andrew
30° Knights Kadosh
31° Grand Inspector Inquisitor Commander
32° Sublime Prince of the Royal Secret

Concordant Bodies and Degrees within the Ancient and Accepted Scottish Rite of Freemasonry of Canada

LODGE OF PERFECTION, 4° - 14°
CHAPTER OF ROSE CROIX, 15° - 18°
CONSISTORY, 19° - 32°
COURT OF HONOR
　　　Knight Commander of the Court of Honour (KCCH)
　　　Grand Cross of the Court of Honour (GCCH)
SUPREME COUNCIL, 33°

DEGREES:

4°　Secret Master
5°　Perfect Master
6°　Intimate Secretary
7°　Provost and Judge
8°　Intendant of the Building
9°　Elect of the Nine
10°　Elect of the Fifteen
11°　Elect of the Twelve
12°　Grand Master Architect
13°　Royal Arch of Solomon
14°　Grand Elect Perfect and Sublime Mason
15°　Knight of the East, or Knight of the Sword
16°　Prince of Jerusalem
17°　Knight of the East and West
18°　Knight Rose Croix
19°　Grand Pontiff
20°　 Master ad Vitam
21°　Patriarch Noachite
22°　Prince of Libanus
23°　Chief of the Tabernacle

24° Prince of the Tabernacle
25° Knight of the Brazen Serpent
26° Prince of Mercy
27° Commander of the Temple
28° Knight of the Sun
29° Knight of Saint Andrew
30° Knight Kadosh
31° Inspector Inquisitor Commander
32° Sublime Prince of the Royal Secret
33° Inspector General

2 COLLEGE OF FREEMASONRY

Throughout the decades since the inception, the Scottish Rite has often been referred to as the College of Freemasonry. In this chapter, we provide a place for you jot down personal notes as you reflect upon your thoughts about each particular degree, what you learned from them, what you have learned from more informed Brethren, how you can benefit from their teachings, and what you drew from them that you could share later in discussions about them with less informed Brothers.

You must first learn and understand the meanings of these valuable teachings, examples, instructions, and advice. This may take hours, days, months or years. The more you reflect and study them, and the more you apply them to your life, the more you will thus improve yourself in Masonry. If you pay your fees, attend a degree festival, and never return to the Valley, you will not know, not understand, and not reap the benefits that lie in the Valley.

Today, more than ever, young men need a place in the Valley. Only with your help, great or small, may they continue to enter the Valley and benefit from the fruits of its labor, but without your assistance, they do not know where to go or what to do once they arrive...or that they need to go there...

Brother, that task falls upon you, young or old, new or seasoned.

4th Degree (4°)

Personal Reflections on this Degree

5th Degree (5°)

Personal Reflections on this Degree

6th Degree (6°)

Personal Reflections on this Degree

7th Degree (7°)

Personal Reflections on this Degree

8th Degree (8°)

Personal Reflections on this Degree

9th Degree (9°)

Personal Reflections on this Degree

10th Degree (10°)

Personal Reflections on this Degree

11th Degree (11°)

Personal Reflections on this Degree

12th Degree (12°)

Personal Reflections on this Degree

_____

_____

_____

_____

_____

_____

_____

_____

_____

_____

_____

_____

_____

_____

_____

_____

_____

13th Degree (13°)

Personal Reflections on this Degree

14th Degree (14°)

Personal Reflections on this Degree

15th Degree (15°)

Personal Reflections on this Degree

16th Degree (16°)

Personal Reflections on this Degree

17th Degree (17°)

Personal Reflections on this Degree

18th Degree (18°)

Personal Reflections on this Degree

19th Degree (19°)

Personal Reflections on this Degree

20th Degree (20°)

Personal Reflections on this Degree

21st Degree (21°)

Personal Reflections on this Degree

22nd Degree (22°)

Personal Reflections on this Degree

_____

_____

_____

_____

_____

_____

_____

_____

_____

_____

_____

_____

_____

_____

_____

_____

23rd Degree (23°)

Personal Reflections on this Degree

24th Degree (24°)

Personal Reflections on this Degree

25th Degree (25°)

Personal Reflections on this Degree

26th Degree (26°)

Personal Reflections on this Degree

27th Degree (27°)

Personal Reflections on this Degree

28th Degree (28°)

Personal Reflections on this Degree

_____

_____

_____

_____

_____

_____

_____

_____

_____

_____

_____

_____

_____

_____

_____

_____

_____

29th Degree (29°)

Personal Reflections on this Degree

30th Degree (30°)

Personal Reflections on this Degree

31st Degree (31°)

Personal Reflections on this Degree

32nd Degree (32°)

Personal Reflections on this Degree

_____

_____

_____

_____

_____

_____

_____

_____

_____

_____

_____

_____

_____

_____

_____

_____

_____

_____

_____

_____

KCCH
Knight Commander of the Court of Honour

At the biennial session of the Supreme Council certain Masters of the Royal Secret, having held that degree for at least forty-six months prior to the session, are chosen to receive the Rank and Decoration of Knights Commander of the Court of Honour. These are chosen from the ranks of the Consistory for special service to Masonry, or to mankind, by the Deputy or Sovereign Grand Inspector General. The Knight Commander of the Court of Honour may be recognized by the red cap they are entitled to wear. The rank of KCCH, if petitioned or asked for, must be refused.

Personal Reflections on this Honour

_____

_____

_____

_____

_____

_____

_____

_____

_____

_____

_____

_____

_____

33rd Degree (33°)
Inspector General Honorary

The Thirty-third Degree is conferred by the Supreme Council upon members of the Rite in recognition of outstanding work in the Rite or in public life. The 33° cannot be asked for and if asked for must be refused. At its bi-ennial session the Supreme Council elects members of the Rite to receive the Degree. These 33° Masons are Inspectors General honorary and honorary members of the Supreme Council. The active members of the Supreme Council are chosen from among them.

Personal Reflections on this Degree

_____

_____

_____

_____

_____

_____

_____

_____

_____

_____

_____

_____

GCCH
Grand Cross of the Court of Honour

This is the highest individual honor that The Supreme Council bestows. It is voted very rarely to Thirty-third Degree Masons only for the most exceptional and extraordinary services. The Grand Cross cap is white with a blue band. On the front is a replica of the Grand Cross jewel, which is composed of a Teutonic Cross, with an embroidered crimson rose with green leaves at its center.

Personal Reflections on this Degree

_____

_____

_____

_____

_____

_____

_____

_____

_____

_____

_____

_____

_____

_____

3 INVITATIONAL & ASSOCIATED BODIES

INVITATIONAL BODY OF THE ANCIENT AND ACCEPTED SCOTTISH RITE

The Royal Order of Scotland occupies a unique place in American Masonry, as it is controlled by the Grand Lodge of Scotland, and was "usurped" in a sense when Albert Pike was appointed the Provincial Grand Master and allied it with the A.A.S.R. However, the statues in the U.S.A. still conform to those of the mother Grand Lodge and the body is open to 32º Scottish Rite Masons by invitation and Knights Templar by special waiver.

The Royal Order of Scotland (ROS)

An invitational body composed of highly dedicated and long serving Scottish Rite Masons. While allied with and considered a Scottish Rite Degree in the United States, this Order was once under the jurisdiction of the York Rite, being controlled by the Grand Lodge of Scotland, and as a result of this former disposition, it is also open to Knights Templar by waiver of the Provincial Grand Master. Membership requires affiliation with the Scottish Rite (32º) and a Trinitarian Christian, or a Knight Templar; and the recommendation of a member.

This is the only Masonic body that is considered to be an

authentic Royal Order. The Degree of Knight of the Rosy Cross is believed to contain remnants of the original investiture ceremony of the Most Ancient and Most Noble Order of the Thistle, the Royal Scottish Dynastic Order. The Masonic body is under the jurisdiction of the Grand Lodge of Scotland. In the United States of America, the body operates as a Provincial Grand Lodge, and the presiding officer is a Provincial Grand Master. It is unlimited in membership.

The two degrees worked are:

- Degree of Heredom of Kilwinning
- Degree of Knight of the Rosy Cross

AFFILIATED ADOPTIVE MASONIC BODIES

These are Masonic organizations whose memberships include both men and women in their bodies. The Scottish Rite is an active participant and supporter in Adoptive Masonic bodies.

The Order of the Amaranth

An Adoptive Masonic organization. The organization was founded in 1873. Membership is limited to Masons, their spouses, and female relatives. It was originally intended to be an additional degree of the Order of the Eastern Star, but was rejected by that organization. It was then set up as a separate organization. Until 1921, members had to be affiliated with the Order of the Eastern Star. The presiding body is a Court, and the presiding female and male officers are a Royal Matron and Royal Patron.

The Order of the Eastern Star (OES)

An Adoptive Masonic organization. The organization was founded in 1857. Membership is limited to Masons, their spouses, and female relatives. Meetings require the presence of a Mason in order to open and transact business. The presiding body is a Chapter, and the presiding female and male officers are a Worthy Matron and Worthy Patron.

Degrees worked are:

- Obedience (Adah)
- Devotion (Ruth)
- Fidelity (Esther)
- Faith (Martha)
- Charity (Electa)

The Order of the White Shrine of Jerusalem

An Adoptive Masonic organization. The organization was founded in 1894. Membership is limited to Masons, their spouses, and female relatives. Members must profess the Christian faith. Meetings require the presence of a Mason in order to open and transact business. The presiding body is a Shrine, and the presiding female and male officers are a High Priestess and Watchman of Shepherds.

Social Order of the Beauceant (S.O.O.B.)

As the wives, widows, mothers, daughters and sisters of Knights Templars, they are the only ladies' fraternal order whose eligibility is determined by the husband's membership in the Commandery.

A new Assembly may be constituted wherever there is an active Commandery of Knights Templar of sufficient size to warrant it, and there are several eligible ladies.

MASONIC YOUTH ORGANIZATIONS

These organizations are youth organizations sponsored and supported by the Masonic bodies. The York Rite is extremely active in its involvement with these groups.

The Order of DeMolay (IODM)

A Masonic youth organization for young men aged 12 to 21 years. Membership does not require family Masonic affiliation, nor does it confer any Masonic membership. The organization is dedicated to providing guidance and development of civic leadership and social values in young men. A side body of the DeMolay is the Order of Knighthood. The presiding body is a Chapter, and the presiding officer is a Master Councilor.

Degrees worked include:

- Initiatory Degree
- DeMolay Degree
- Degree of Chevalier (Honorary Degree)

The Order of Job's Daughters (IOJD)

A Masonic youth organization for young women aged 10 to 20 years. Membership is limited to girls with a male Masonic relative. The organization is dedicated to the development of civic leadership and social values in young women. The presiding body is a Bethel, and the presiding officer is an Honored Queen.

Iinitiation ceremony that is separated into three "epochs":

- First Epoch
- Second Epoch
- Third Epoch

The Order of the Rainbow for Girls (IORG)

A Masonic youth organization for young women aged 12 to 20 years. Membership does not require Masonic affiliation, nor does it confer Masonic membership. The organization is dedicated to the development of civic leadership and social values in young women. The presiding body is an Assembly, and the presiding officer is a Worthy Advisor. There is one main degree, that of the Initiation Degree, and one honorary degree, that of the Grand Cross of Colors Degree.

ADDITIONAL MASONIC ORGANIZATIONS

The following lists some of the additional Masonic organizations found in the Masonic family. Included are the bodies of Adoptive Masonry and Masonic sponsored youth organizations.

It does not list the other organizations allied to Masonry such as the AAONMS, Shriners, Daughters of the Nile, Tall Cedars of Lebanon, or Grotto.

Research and Fellowship Bodies

These bodies are open in membership to any Mason. They exist as Masonic research and social fellowship groups.

The Philalethes Society

A Masonic research society that is open to Masons and is dedicated to Masonic research. This body includes many noted Masonic authors and researchers. The presiding body is the Society, and the presiding officer is a President.

The Grand College of Rites of the United States of America

A Masonic research society that is open to Master Masons and is dedicated to the study, history, and preservation of extinct Masonic Rites, rituals, and ceremonies. The membership of this body is predominately composed of York Rite Masons. The body gathers annually for the transaction of business and the presentation of papers. The presiding body is the Grand College, and the presiding officer is a Grand Chancellor (titled Most Illustrious).

The Society of Blue Friars

An invitational Masonic literary body whose membership is composed solely of published Masonic authors, and limited to 20 members. It is unique in its honorary status, there being no fees or membership dues assessed, and its members retain membership ad vita. The presiding body is the Society and the presiding officer is a Grand Abbot (titled Most Illustrious).

The Masonic Order of the Bath

Qualifications for membership:

1) You must be a Master Mason in good standing in Lodges recognized as "regular."
2) There IS NO #2.

The presiding officer is titled "Most Honorable Commander-General". Generally meets in Washington DC as part of Masonic Week.

The High Twelve International

A Masonic luncheon club, open to Masons currently expanded to three Countries. The name of the organization derives from a Masonic term meaning noon. Its stated purpose is to inculcate the ideals taught in Masonry by uniting in the happy bonds of a fraternal hour, those ideals being the strengthening of Masonic ties, participation in community activities, and the furtherance of the public school system. There are no degrees, ritual, or ceremonies. It fulfills the role of the "Table Lodges" found in some jurisdictions, but without the formality or ritual associated with those organizations. The presiding body is a Club, and the presiding officer is a President

Historical Invitational Bodies

These bodies preserve the unique Masonic history and heritage associated with colonial and early American Masonry.

The National Sojourners, Inc.

An invitational body composed of Masons who are or were commissioned, warrant, or senior non-commissioned officers in the Armed Forces of the United States of America, and dedicated to the preservation and perpetuation of the Masonic fraternal heritage and its history in the Armed Forces of the United States of America. Provisions exist for the admission of honorary members who do not meet the prerequisite qualifications.

This body inculcates the principles of the former English and American "military" Lodges, which operated under lawful Craft warrants from the 1700's through the early 1900's. The Grand Lodge of the Philippines was organized as a result of the efforts and work of this body. A side body of the Sojourners is the Heroes of '76. The presiding body is a Chapter, and the presiding officer is a President.

NON-ASSOCIATED YORK RITE BODIES

ROYAL ARCH MASONRY

Mark Master Degree
Past Master Degree
Most Excellent Master Degree
Royal Arch Degree

CRYPTIC MASONRY

Royal Master Degree
Select Master Degree
Super Excellent Master Degree

TEMPLARY

Illustrious Order of the Red Cross
  Knight of the Red Cross

Order of Malta
  Order of St. Paul and the Mediterranean Pass
  Ancient and Masonic Order of St. John of Jerusalem,
    Palestine, Rhodes and Malta

Order of the Temple
  Knight Templar

INVITATIONAL BODIES

THE CHAIR DEGREES

The Order of High Priesthood
Thrice Illustrious Master
Knight Crusader of the Cross
Sovereign Order of Knights Preceptors
Past Commander Associations

APPENDANT AND ALLIED BODIES

Unrestricted Invitational Appendant Bodies
York Rite Sovereign College of North America
The Order of Knight Masons U.S.A.
The Knights of the York Cross of Honour
Commemorative Order of St. Thomas of Acon

Restrictive Invitational Appendant Bodies
Allied Masonic Degrees
Red Cross of Constantine
Holy Royal Arch Knight Templar Priests

4 MASONIC FORMS OF ADDRESS

With such diverseness within the content of the various bodies of the York and Scottish Rite bodies, there comes a confusion as to who is who. This chapter lists the various titles of office within the primary bodies and provides their basic operating hierarchies.

GRAND LODGE OF FREEMASONS

GRAND OFFICER TITLES

Most Worshipful Grand Master
Right Worshipful Deputy Grand Master
Right Worshipful Senior Grand Warden
Right Worshipful Junior Grand Warden
Most Worshipful Past Grand Master
Right Worshipful Grand Treasurer
Right Worshipful Grand Secretary
Right Worshipful Grand Chaplain
Worshipful Senior Grand Deacon
Worshipful Junior Grand Deacon
Worshipful Grand Marshal
Worshipful Grand Sword Bearer
Worshipful Grand Steward
Worshipful Grand Pursuivant

Worshipful Grand Tyler
Worshipful Grand Historian
Worshipful Grand Organist
Worshipful Grand Photographer
Worshipful Grand Lecturer
Past Worshipful Master

LOCAL BODY TITLES

Worshipful Master
Senior Warden
Junior Warden
Treasurer
Past Worshipful Master
Secretary
Chaplain
Senior Deacon
Junior Deacon
Tyler
Marshal
Trustees

ANCIENT & ACCEPTED SCOTTISH RITE

GRAND OFFICER TITLES

Sovereign Grand Commander
Sovereign Grand Inspector General (SGIG)
Deputy Inspector General

LOCAL BODY TITLES

Personal Representative of SGIG
Venerable Master - Lodge of Perfection
Assistant Representative of the Deputy
Wise Master – Chapter of Rose Croix
Preceptor – Council of Kadosh
Master of Kadosh

Executive Secretary
Treasurer
Almoner
Director Extension
Tyler

SCOTTISH RITE HONORS

KCCH – Knight Commander Court of Honor
33rd Degree
Grand Cross of the Court of Honor

GRAND CHAPTER, ROYAL ARCH MASONS

GRAND OFFICER TITLES

Most Excellent Grand High Priest
Right Excellent Grand King
Right Excellent Grand Scribe
Most Excellent Past Grand High Priest
Right Excellent Grand Treasurer
Right Excellent Grand Secretary
Right Excellent Grand Chaplain
Excellent Grand Captain of the Host
Excellent Grand Principal Sojourner
Excellent Grand Royal Arch Captain
Excellent Grand Master of the 1st veil
Excellent Grand Master of the 2nd Veil
Excellent Grand Master of the 3rd veil
Grand Sentinel
District Deputy Grand High Priests

LOCAL BODY TITLES

High Priest
King
Scribe

Past High Priest
Treasurer
Secretary
Chaplain
Captain of the Host
Principal Sojourner
Royal Arch Captain
Master of the 1st veil
Master of the 2nd Veil
Master of the 3rd veil
Sentinel
Key Man

GRAND COUNCIL, CRYPTIC MASONS (ROYAL & SELECT MASTERS)

GRAND OFFICER TITLES

Most Illustrious Grand Master
Right Illustrious Deputy Grand Master
Right Illustrious Grand Principal Conductor of the Work
Most Illustrious Past Grand Master
Right Illustrious Grand Treasurer
Right Illustrious Grand Recorder
Illustrious Grand Captain of the Guard
Illustrious Grand Conductor of the Council
Illustrious Grand Steward
Illustrious Grand Chaplain
Illustrious Grand Marshal
Illustrious Grand Sentinel
Grand Masters Personal Representatives
Grand Instructors

LOCAL BODY TITLES

Illustrious Master
Deputy Master
Principal Conductor of the Work

Past Illustrious Master
Treasurer
Recorder
Captain of the Guard
Conductor of the Council
Steward
Chaplain
Marshal
Sentinel
Key Man

GRAND COMMANDERY, KNIGHTS TEMPLAR

GRAND OFFICER TITLES

Right Eminent Grand Commander
Very Eminent Deputy Grand Commander
Eminent Grand Generalissimo
Eminent Grand Captain General
Right Eminent Past Grand Commander
Eminent Grand Senior Warden
Eminent Grand Junior Warden
Eminent Grand Prelate
Eminent Grand Treasurer
Eminent Grand Recorder
Eminent Grand Standard Bearer
Eminent Grand Sword Bearer
Eminent Grand Warder
Eminent Grand Sentinel
Past Grand Department Commander

LOCAL BODY TITLES

Eminent Commander
Generalissimo
Captain General
Past Commander
Senior Warden

Junior Warden
Prelate
Treasurer
Recorder
Standard Bearer
Sword Bearer
Warder
Sentinel
Guard (x3)

GRAND ENCAMPMENT, KNIGHTS TEMPLAR

Most Eminent Grand Master
Right Eminent Deputy Grand Master
Right Eminent Grand Generalissimo
Right Eminent Grand Captain General
Most Eminent Past Grand Master
Right Eminent Grand Senior Warden
Right Eminent Grand Junior Warden
Right Eminent Grand Prelate
Right Eminent Grand Treasurer
Right Eminent Grand Recorder
Right Eminent Grand Standard Bearer
Right Eminent Grand Sword Bearer
Right Eminent Grand Warder
Right Eminent Grand Sentinel
Right Eminent Grand Marshal
Right Eminent Deprtment Commander
Right Eminent Past Grand Officer
Right Eminent Past Department Commander

YORK RITE COLLEGE (YRC)

GRAND OFFICER TITLES

Past Grand Governor
Grand Governor

Deputy Grand Governor
Deputy Grand Governor

LOCAL BODY TITLES

Past Eminent Governor
Preeminent Governor
Eminent Deputy Governor
Eminent Chancellor
Eminent Treasurer
Eminent Secretary
Noble Primate
Noble Preceptor
Noble Seneschal
Noble Marshal
Noble Sentinel

GRAND COUNCIL, KNIGHTS MASON, USA

KCZ – Knight Commander of Zerubbabel (Honor)

GRAND OFFICER TITLES

Most Excellent Past Grand Chief
Most Excellent Grand Chief
Right Excellent Deputy Grand Chief
Right Excellent Grand Senior Warden
Right Excellent Junior Warden
Right Excellent Grand Scribe
Right Excellent Grand Treasurer
Very Excellent Grand Senior Warden
Very Excellent Junior Warden
Very Excellent Grand Director of Ceremonies
Very Excellent Grand Priest
Very Excellent Grand Steward
Very Excellent Grand Sentinel
Right Excellent Grand Musician
Excellent Chief of Great Chief's

LOCAL BODY TITLES

Excellent Chief
Senior Knight
Junior Knight
Secretary
Treasurer
Senior Warden
Junior Warden
Director of Ceremonies
Priest
First Guard
Sentinel

ACRONYMS for YORK RITE HONORS

GRAND OFFICER TITLES

KCC – Knight Crusader of the Cross
KCT – Knight Commander of the Temple
KGC – Knight Grand Cross (Grand Encampment)
KTCH – Knight Templar Cross of Honor
KYCH – Knight York Cross of Honor
KYGCH – Knight York Grand Cross of Honor

LOCAL BODY TITLES

RCC – Red Cross of Constantine
RIC – Rosicrucian (Societas Rosicruciana)
ROS – Royal Order of Scotland
RTB – Robert The Bruce
OPC – Order of the Purple Cross
4BL – Order of the Four Black Lamas (For fun)

ALLIED MASONIC DEGREES

GRAND OFFICER TITLES

Past Sovereign Grand Master
Sovereign Grand Master
Knight Grand Cross
Knight Branch of Eri
Sovereign Master
Supreme Ruler of the Secret Monitor
Worshipful Master-St. Lawrence the Martyr
Commander Noah-Royal Ark Mariner

LOCAL BODY TITLES

Sovereign Master
Senior Warden
Junior Warden
Senior Deacon
Junior Deacon
Chaplain
Secretary
Treasurer
Tyler

CONVENT GENERAL - KYCH

GRAND OFFICER TITLES

Grand Master General
Deputy Grand Master-General
Grand Warder of the Temple
Past Grand Master General
Grand Treasurer-General
Grand Registrar-General
Grand Seneschal
Grand Marshal
Grand Sentinel

Grand Prelate
LOCAL BODY TITLES (PRIORY)

Eminent Prior
Deputy Prior
Warder
Past Prior
Registrar-Treasurer
Prelate
Orator
Herald

GRAND COUNCIL
ORDER of HIGH PRIESTHOOD

Most Excellent Grand President
Most Excellent Grand Vice President
Most Excellent Grand Chaplain
Most Excellent Grand Recorder-Treasurer
Most Excellent Master of Ceremonies
Most Excellent Grand Conductor
Most Excellent Grand Herald
Most Excellent Grand Steward
Most Excellent Grand Sentinel
Most Excellent Past Grand President

ORDER OF THE SILVER TROWEL

Illustrious King
Illustrious Prince of the West
Illustrious Prince of the South
Illustrious Treasurer-Scribe
Illustrious Prince of the Court
Illustrious Captain of the Guard
Illustrious Chaplain
Past Illustrious King

SHRINE

Illustrious Potentate
Chief Rabban
Assistant Rabban
Past Illustrious Potentate
High Priest and Prophet
Oriental Guide
Treasurer
Recorder

STRUCTURE & ORGANIZATION OF FREEMASONRY

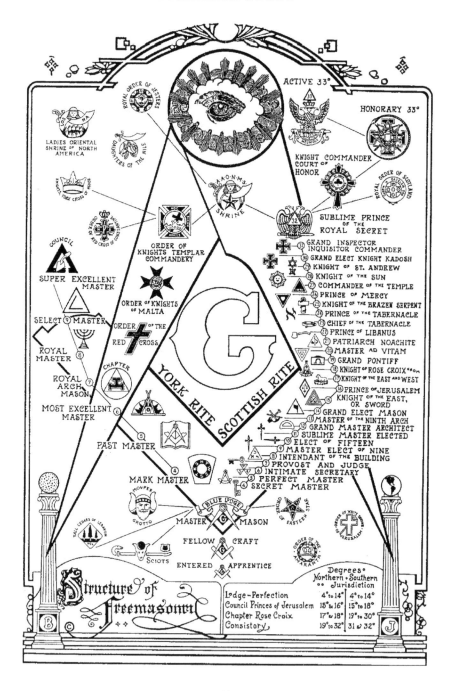

5 SCOTTISH RITE DEGREE RECORD

Presented_____   **Elected**_____

Lodge_____ **No.**_____

THE SYMBOLIC DEGREES (CRAFT/BLUE LODGE)

Entered Apprentice

Date_____ Location_____

Body_____ No. _____

Fellow Craft

Date_____ Location_____

Body_____ No. _____

Master Mason

Date_____ Location_____

Body_____ No. _____

LODGE OF PERFECTION DEGREES

Date_____

In _____ Lodge of Perfection

Valley_____

CHAPTER DEGREES

Date_____

In _____ Chapter of Rose Croix

Valley_____

COUNCIL DEGREES

Date_____

In _____ Council of Kadosh

Valley_____

CONSISTORY DEGREES

Date_____

In _____ Consistory

Valley_____

The Masonic Order of the Bath

Date_____ Location_____

Body_____ No. _____

The Royal Order of Scotland (ROS)

Degree of Heredom of Kilwinning

Date_____ Location_____

Body_____ No. _____

Degree of Knight of the Rosy Cross

Date_____ Location_____

Body_____ No. _____

6 OTHER DEGREES RECORD

You may use this space to record degrees that you have received that are not otherwise listed in this book, i.e, York Rite, Shrine, OES, Order of the Aramanth, Grotto, etc.

Degree_____

Date_____ Location_____

Body_____ No. _____

Degree_____

Date_____ Location_____

Body_____ No. _____

Degree_____

Date_____ Location_____

Body_____ No. _____

Degree_____

Date_____ Location_____

Body_____ No. _____

Degree_____

Date_____ Location_____

Body_____ No. _____

Degree_____

Date_____ Location_____

Body_____ No. _____

Degree_____

Date_____ Location_____

Body_____ No. _____

Degree_____

Date_____ Location_____

Body_____ No. _____

Degree_____

Date_____ Location_____

Body_____ No. _____

Degree_____

Date_____ Location_____

Body_____ No. _____

Degree_____

Date_____ Location_____

Body_____ No. _____

Degree_____

Date_____ Location_____

Body_____ No. _____

Degree_____

Date_____ Location_____

Body_____ No. _____

Degree_____

Date_____ Location_____

Body_____ No. _____

Degree_____

Date_____ Location_____

Body_____ No. _____

Degree_____

Date_____ Location_____

Body_____ No. _____

Degree_____

Date_____ Location_____

Body_____ No. _____

Degree_____

Date_____ Location_____

Body_____ No. _____

Degree_____

Date_____ Location_____

Body_____ No. _____

Degree_____

Date_____ Location_____

Body_____ No. _____

Degree_____

Date_____ Location_____

Body_____ No. _____

Degree_____

Date_____ Location_____

Body_____ No. _____

Degree_____

Date_____ Location_____

Body_____ No. _____

Degree_____

Date_____ Location_____

Body_____ No. _____

Degree_____

Date_____ Location_____

Body_____ No. _____

Degree_____

Date_____ Location_____

Body_____ No. _____

Degree_____

Date_____ Location_____

Body_____ No. _____

Degree_____

Date_____ Location_____

Body_____ No. _____

Degree_____

Date_____ Location_____

Body_____ No. _____

Degree_____

Date_____ Location_____

Body_____ No. _____

Degree_____

Date_____ Location_____

Body_____ No. _____

Degree_____

Date_____ Location_____

Body_____ No. _____

Degree_____

Date_____ Location_____

Body_____ No. _____

Degree_____

Date_____ Location_____

Body_____ No. _____

Degree_____

Date_____ Location_____

Body_____ No. _____

Degree_____

Date_____ Location_____

Body_____ No. _____

Degree_____

Date_____ Location_____

Body_____ No. _____

Degree_____

Date_____ Location_____

Body_____ No. _____

Degree_____

Date_____ Location_____

Body_____ No. _____

Degree_____

Date_____ Location_____

Body_____ No. _____

Degree_____

Date_____ Location_____

Body_____ No. _____

Degree_____

Date_____ Location_____

Body_____ No. _____

Degree_____

Date_____ Location_____

Body_____ No. _____

Degree_____

Date_____ Location_____

Body_____ No. _____

Degree_____

Date_____ Location_____

Body_____ No. _____

Degree_____

Date_____ Location_____

Body_____ No. _____

Degree_____

Date_____ Location_____

Body_____ No. _____

Degree_____

Date_____ Location_____

Body_____ No. _____

Degree_____

Date_____ Location_____

Body_____ No. _____

Degree_____

Date_____ Location_____

Body_____ No. _____

Degree_____

Date_____ Location_____

Body_____ No. _____

Degree_____

Date_____ Location_____

Body_____ No. _____

Degree_____

Date_____ Location_____

Body_____ No. _____

Degree_____

Date_____ Location_____

Body_____ No. _____

Degree_____

Date_____ Location_____

Body_____ No. _____

Degree_____

Date_____ Location_____

Body_____ No. _____

Degree_____

Date_____ Location_____

Body_____ No. _____

7 OFFICES HELD

You may list the offices, dates, and special appointments you have held in various Masonic bodies. If you are actively involved in several bodies, you will want to record your service and progression through the ranks. This serves as a backup record and personal tracker for you.

BODY_____

Dates   Office Held/Appointment Received

_____   _____

_____   _____

_____   _____

_____   _____

_____   _____

_____   _____

_____   _____

_____   _____

_____   _____

_____   _____

_____   _____

_____   _____

_____   _____

_____   _____

_____   _____

_____   _____

BODY_____

Dates

Office Held/Appointment Received

_____   _____

_____   _____

_____   _____

_____   _____

_____   _____

_____   _____

_____   _____

_____   _____

_____   _____

_____   _____

_____   _____

_____   _____

_____   _____

_____   _____

_____   _____

BODY

Dates	Office Held/Appointment Received

BODY_____

Dates   Office Held/Appointment Received

_____   _____

_____   _____

_____   _____

_____   _____

_____   _____

_____   _____

_____   _____

_____   _____

_____   _____

_____   _____

_____   _____

_____   _____

_____   _____

_____   _____

_____   _____

BODY

Dates

Office Held/Appointment Received

_____ _____

_____ _____

_____ _____

_____ _____

_____ _____

_____ _____

_____ _____

_____ _____

_____ _____

_____ _____

_____ _____

_____ _____

_____ _____

_____ _____

_____ _____

_____ _____

BODY

Dates	Office Held/Appointment Received

BODY

Dates   Office Held/Appointment Received

_____   _____

_____   _____

_____   _____

_____   _____

_____   _____

_____   _____

_____   _____

_____   _____

_____   _____

_____   _____

_____   _____

_____   _____

_____   _____

_____   _____

BODY

Dates	Office Held/Appointment Received
_____	_____
_____	_____
_____	_____
_____	_____
_____	_____
_____	_____
_____	_____
_____	_____
_____	_____
_____	_____
_____	_____
_____	_____
_____	_____
_____	_____
_____	_____
_____	_____
_____	_____

BODY

Dates	Office Held/Appointment Received

BODY_____

Dates   Office Held/Appointment Received

_____   _____

_____   _____

_____   _____

_____   _____

_____

_____   _____

_____   _____

_____   _____

_____   _____

_____   _____

_____   _____

_____   _____

_____   _____

_____   _____

_____   _____

BODY

Dates   Office Held/Appointment Received

_____   _____

_____   _____

_____   _____

_____   _____

_____   _____

_____   _____

_____   _____

_____   _____

_____   _____

_____   _____

_____   _____

_____   _____

_____   _____

_____   _____

_____   _____

BODY

Dates   Office Held/Appointment Received

_____   _____

_____   _____

_____   _____

_____   _____

_____   _____

_____   _____

_____   _____

_____   _____

_____   _____

_____   _____

_____   _____

_____   _____

_____   _____

_____   _____

_____   _____

BODY_____

Dates   Office Held/Appointment Received

_____   _____

_____   _____

_____   _____

_____   _____

_____   _____

_____   _____

_____   _____

_____   _____

_____   _____

_____   _____

_____   _____

_____   _____

_____   _____

_____   _____

_____   _____

_____   _____

_____   _____

BODY

Dates   Office Held/Appointment Received

_____   _____

_____   _____

_____   _____

_____   _____

_____   _____

_____   _____

_____   _____

_____   _____

_____   _____

_____   _____

_____   _____

_____   _____

_____   _____

_____   _____

_____   _____

BODY

Dates	Office Held/Appointment Received
_____	_____
_____	_____
_____	_____
_____	_____
_____	_____
_____	_____
_____	_____
_____	_____
_____	_____
_____	_____
_____	_____
_____	_____
_____	_____
_____	_____
_____	_____
_____	_____

BODY_____

Dates   Office Held/Appointment Received

_____   _____

_____   _____

_____   _____

_____   _____

_____   _____

_____   _____

_____   _____

_____   _____

_____   _____

_____   _____

_____   _____

_____   _____

_____   _____

_____   _____

_____   _____

BODY

Dates   Office Held/Appointment Received

_____   _____

_____   _____

_____   _____

_____   _____

_____   _____

_____   _____

_____   _____

_____   _____

_____   _____

_____   _____

_____   _____

_____   _____

_____   _____

_____   _____

_____   _____

_____   _____

_____   _____

BODY

Dates	Office Held/Appointment Received
_____	_____
_____	_____
_____	_____
_____	_____
_____	_____
_____	_____
_____	_____
_____	_____
_____	_____
_____	_____
_____	_____
_____	_____
_____	_____
_____	_____
_____	_____
_____	_____
_____	_____

BODY

Dates   Office Held/Appointment Received

_____   _____

_____   _____

_____   _____

_____   _____

_____   _____

_____   _____

_____   _____

_____   _____

_____   _____

_____   _____

_____   _____

_____   _____

_____   _____

_____   _____

_____   _____

_____   _____

8 DEGREE WORK/ATTENDANCE

In this section you may list the various degree work you have attended and/or worked in for the various Masonic bodies you are involved with.

DEGREE_____

Date	Location	Worked?
_____	_____	❑ Y ❑ N
_____	_____	❑ Y ❑ N
_____	_____	❑ Y ❑ N
_____	_____	❑ Y ❑ N
_____	_____	❑ Y ❑ N
_____	_____	❑ Y ❑ N
_____	_____	❑ Y ❑ N
_____	_____	❑ Y ❑ N
_____	_____	❑ Y ❑ N
_____	_____	❑ Y ❑ N
_____	_____	❑ Y ❑ N
_____	_____	❑ Y ❑ N
_____	_____	❑ Y ❑ N
_____	_____	❑ Y ❑ N
_____	_____	❑ Y ❑ N
_____	_____	❑ Y ❑ N
_____	_____	❑ Y ❑ N
_____	_____	❑ Y ❑ N

DEGREE_____

Date	Location	Worked?
_____	_____	❏ Y ❏ N
_____	_____	❏ Y ❏ N
_____	_____	❏ Y ❏ N
_____	_____	❏ Y ❏ N
_____	_____	❏ Y ❏ N
_____	_____	❏ Y ❏ N
_____	_____	❏ Y ❏ N
_____	_____	❏ Y ❏ N
_____	_____	❏ Y ❏ N
_____	_____	❏ Y ❏ N
_____	_____	❏ Y ❏ N
_____	_____	❏ Y ❏ N
_____	_____	❏ Y ❏ N
_____	_____	❏ Y ❏ N
_____	_____	❏ Y ❏ N
_____	_____	❏ Y ❏ N
_____	_____	❏ Y ❏ N
_____	_____	❏ Y ❏ N

DEGREE_____

Date	Location	Worked?
_____	_____	❏ Y ❏ N
_____	_____	❏ Y ❏ N
_____	_____	❏ Y ❏ N
_____	_____	❏ Y ❏ N
_____	_____	❏ Y ❏ N
_____	_____	❏ Y ❏ N
_____	_____	❏ Y ❏ N
_____	_____	❏ Y ❏ N
_____	_____	❏ Y ❏ N
_____	_____	❏ Y ❏ N
_____	_____	❏ Y ❏ N
_____	_____	❏ Y ❏ N
_____	_____	❏ Y ❏ N
_____	_____	❏ Y ❏ N
_____	_____	❏ Y ❏ N
_____	_____	❏ Y ❏ N
_____	_____	❏ Y ❏ N
_____	_____	❏ Y ❏ N

DEGREE_____

Date	Location	Worked?
_____	_____	❏ Y ❏ N
_____	_____	❏ Y ❏ N
_____	_____	❏ Y ❏ N
_____	_____	❏ Y ❏ N
_____	_____	❏ Y ❏ N
_____	_____	❏ Y ❏ N
_____	_____	❏ Y ❏ N
_____	_____	❏ Y ❏ N
_____	_____	❏ Y ❏ N
_____	_____	❏ Y ❏ N
_____	_____	❏ Y ❏ N
_____	_____	❏ Y ❏ N
_____	_____	❏ Y ❏ N
_____	_____	❏ Y ❏ N
_____	_____	❏ Y ❏ N
_____	_____	❏ Y ❏ N
_____	_____	❏ Y ❏ N
_____	_____	❏ Y ❏ N

DEGREE_____

Date	Location	Worked?
_____	_____	❏ Y ❏ N
_____	_____	❏ Y ❏ N
_____	_____	❏ Y ❏ N
_____	_____	❏ Y ❏ N
_____	_____	❏ Y ❏ N
_____	_____	❏ Y ❏ N
_____	_____	❏ Y ❏ N
_____	_____	❏ Y ❏ N
_____	_____	❏ Y ❏ N
_____	_____	❏ Y ❏ N
_____	_____	❏ Y ❏ N
_____	_____	❏ Y ❏ N
_____	_____	❏ Y ❏ N
_____	_____	❏ Y ❏ N
_____	_____	❏ Y ❏ N
_____	_____	❏ Y ❏ N
_____	_____	❏ Y ❏ N
_____	_____	❏ Y ❏ N

DEGREE_____

Date	Location	Worked?
_____	_____	❏ Y ❏ N
_____	_____	❏ Y ❏ N
_____	_____	❏ Y ❏ N
_____	_____	❏ Y ❏ N
_____	_____	❏ Y ❏ N
_____	_____	❏ Y ❏ N
_____	_____	❏ Y ❏ N
_____	_____	❏ Y ❏ N
_____	_____	❏ Y ❏ N
_____	_____	❏ Y ❏ N
_____	_____	❏ Y ❏ N
_____	_____	❏ Y ❏ N
_____	_____	❏ Y ❏ N
_____	_____	❏ Y ❏ N
_____	_____	❏ Y ❏ N
_____	_____	❏ Y ❏ N
_____	_____	❏ Y ❏ N
_____	_____	❏ Y ❏ N

DEGREE_____

Date	Location	Worked?
_____	_____	❑ Y ❑ N
_____	_____	❑ Y ❑ N
_____	_____	❑ Y ❑ N
_____	_____	❑ Y ❑ N
_____	_____	❑ Y ❑ N
_____	_____	❑ Y ❑ N
_____	_____	❑ Y ❑ N
_____	_____	❑ Y ❑ N
_____	_____	❑ Y ❑ N
_____	_____	❑ Y ❑ N
_____	_____	❑ Y ❑ N
_____	_____	❑ Y ❑ N
_____	_____	❑ Y ❑ N
_____	_____	❑ Y ❑ N
_____	_____	❑ Y ❑ N
_____	_____	❑ Y ❑ N
_____	_____	❑ Y ❑ N
_____	_____	❑ Y ❑ N

DEGREE_____

Date	Location	Worked?
_____	_____	❏ Y ❏ N
_____	_____	❏ Y ❏ N
_____	_____	❏ Y ❏ N
_____	_____	❏ Y ❏ N
_____	_____	❏ Y ❏ N
_____	_____	❏ Y ❏ N
_____	_____	❏ Y ❏ N
_____	_____	❏ Y ❏ N
_____	_____	❏ Y ❏ N
_____	_____	❏ Y ❏ N
_____	_____	❏ Y ❏ N
_____	_____	❏ Y ❏ N
_____	_____	❏ Y ❏ N
_____	_____	❏ Y ❏ N
_____	_____	❏ Y ❏ N
_____	_____	❏ Y ❏ N
_____	_____	❏ Y ❏ N
_____	_____	❏ Y ❏ N

DEGREE_____

Date	Location	Worked?
_____	_____	❑ Y ❑ N
_____	_____	❑ Y ❑ N
_____	_____	❑ Y ❑ N
_____	_____	❑ Y ❑ N
_____	_____	❑ Y ❑ N
_____	_____	❑ Y ❑ N
_____	_____	❑ Y ❑ N
_____	_____	❑ Y ❑ N
_____	_____	❑ Y ❑ N
_____	_____	❑ Y ❑ N
_____	_____	❑ Y ❑ N
_____	_____	❑ Y ❑ N
_____	_____	❑ Y ❑ N
_____	_____	❑ Y ❑ N
_____	_____	❑ Y ❑ N
_____	_____	❑ Y ❑ N
_____	_____	❑ Y ❑ N
_____	_____	❑ Y ❑ N

DEGREE_____

Date	Location	Worked?
_____	_____	❏ Y ❏ N
_____	_____	❏ Y ❏ N
_____	_____	❏ Y ❏ N
_____	_____	❏ Y ❏ N
_____	_____	❏ Y ❏ N
_____	_____	❏ Y ❏ N
_____	_____	❏ Y ❏ N
_____	_____	❏ Y ❏ N
_____	_____	❏ Y ❏ N
_____	_____	❏ Y ❏ N
_____	_____	❏ Y ❏ N
_____	_____	❏ Y ❏ N
_____	_____	❏ Y ❏ N
_____	_____	❏ Y ❏ N
_____	_____	❏ Y ❏ N
_____	_____	❏ Y ❏ N
_____	_____	❏ Y ❏ N
_____	_____	❏ Y ❏ N

DEGREE_____

Date	Location	Worked?
_____	_____	❏ Y ❏ N
_____	_____	❏ Y ❏ N
_____	_____	❏ Y ❏ N
_____	_____	❏ Y ❏ N
_____	_____	❏ Y ❏ N
_____	_____	❏ Y ❏ N
_____	_____	❏ Y ❏ N
_____	_____	❏ Y ❏ N
_____	_____	❏ Y ❏ N
_____	_____	❏ Y ❏ N
_____	_____	❏ Y ❏ N
_____	_____	❏ Y ❏ N
_____	_____	❏ Y ❏ N
_____	_____	❏ Y ❏ N
_____	_____	❏ Y ❏ N
_____	_____	❏ Y ❏ N
_____	_____	❏ Y ❏ N
_____	_____	❏ Y ❏ N

DEGREE_____

Date	Location	Worked?
_____	_____	❏ Y ❏ N
_____	_____	❏ Y ❏ N
_____	_____	❏ Y ❏ N
_____	_____	❏ Y ❏ N
_____	_____	❏ Y ❏ N
_____	_____	❏ Y ❏ N
_____	_____	❏ Y ❏ N
_____	_____	❏ Y ❏ N
_____	_____	❏ Y ❏ N
_____	_____	❏ Y ❏ N
_____	_____	❏ Y ❏ N
_____	_____	❏ Y ❏ N
_____	_____	❏ Y ❏ N
_____	_____	❏ Y ❏ N
_____	_____	❏ Y ❏ N
_____	_____	❏ Y ❏ N
_____	_____	❏ Y ❏ N
_____	_____	❏ Y ❏ N

DEGREE_____

Date	Location	Worked?
_____	_____	❏ Y ❏ N
_____	_____	❏ Y ❏ N
_____	_____	❏ Y ❏ N
_____	_____	❏ Y ❏ N
_____	_____	❏ Y ❏ N
_____	_____	❏ Y ❏ N
_____	_____	❏ Y ❏ N
_____	_____	❏ Y ❏ N
_____	_____	❏ Y ❏ N
_____	_____	❏ Y ❏ N
_____	_____	❏ Y ❏ N
_____	_____	❏ Y ❏ N
_____	_____	❏ Y ❏ N
_____	_____	❏ Y ❏ N
_____	_____	❏ Y ❏ N
_____	_____	❏ Y ❏ N
_____	_____	❏ Y ❏ N
_____	_____	❏ Y ❏ N

DEGREE_____

Date	Location	Worked?
_____	_____	❏ Y ❏ N
_____	_____	❏ Y ❏ N
_____	_____	❏ Y ❏ N
_____	_____	❏ Y ❏ N
_____	_____	❏ Y ❏ N
_____	_____	❏ Y ❏ N
_____	_____	❏ Y ❏ N
_____	_____	❏ Y ❏ N
_____	_____	❏ Y ❏ N
_____	_____	❏ Y ❏ N
_____	_____	❏ Y ❏ N
_____	_____	❏ Y ❏ N
_____	_____	❏ Y ❏ N
_____	_____	❏ Y ❏ N
_____	_____	❏ Y ❏ N
_____	_____	❏ Y ❏ N
_____	_____	❏ Y ❏ N
_____	_____	❏ Y ❏ N

DEGREE_____

Date	Location	Worked?
_____	_____	❑ Y ❑ N
_____	_____	❑ Y ❑ N
_____	_____	❑ Y ❑ N
_____	_____	❑ Y ❑ N
_____	_____	❑ Y ❑ N
_____	_____	❑ Y ❑ N
_____	_____	❑ Y ❑ N
_____	_____	❑ Y ❑ N
_____	_____	❑ Y ❑ N
_____	_____	❑ Y ❑ N
_____	_____	❑ Y ❑ N
_____	_____	❑ Y ❑ N
_____	_____	❑ Y ❑ N
_____	_____	❑ Y ❑ N
_____	_____	❑ Y ❑ N
_____	_____	❑ Y ❑ N
_____	_____	❑ Y ❑ N
_____	_____	❑ Y ❑ N

DEGREE_____

Date	Location	Worked?
_____	_____	❑ Y ❑ N
_____	_____	❑ Y ❑ N
_____	_____	❑ Y ❑ N
_____	_____	❑ Y ❑ N
_____	_____	❑ Y ❑ N
_____	_____	❑ Y ❑ N
_____	_____	❑ Y ❑ N
_____	_____	❑ Y ❑ N
_____	_____	❑ Y ❑ N
_____	_____	❑ Y ❑ N
_____	_____	❑ Y ❑ N
_____	_____	❑ Y ❑ N
_____	_____	❑ Y ❑ N
_____	_____	❑ Y ❑ N
_____	_____	❑ Y ❑ N
_____	_____	❑ Y ❑ N
_____	_____	❑ Y ❑ N
_____	_____	❑ Y ❑ N

DEGREE_____

Date	Location	Worked?
_____	_____	❑ Y ❑ N
_____	_____	❑ Y ❑ N
_____	_____	❑ Y ❑ N
_____	_____	❑ Y ❑ N
_____	_____	❑ Y ❑ N
_____	_____	❑ Y ❑ N
_____	_____	❑ Y ❑ N
_____	_____	❑ Y ❑ N
_____	_____	❑ Y ❑ N
_____	_____	❑ Y ❑ N
_____	_____	❑ Y ❑ N
_____	_____	❑ Y ❑ N
_____	_____	❑ Y ❑ N
_____	_____	❑ Y ❑ N
_____	_____	❑ Y ❑ N
_____	_____	❑ Y ❑ N
_____	_____	❑ Y ❑ N
_____	_____	❑ Y ❑ N

DEGREE _____

Date	Location	Worked?
_____	_____	❏ Y ❏ N
_____	_____	❏ Y ❏ N
_____	_____	❏ Y ❏ N
_____	_____	❏ Y ❏ N
		❏ Y ❏ N
_____	_____	❏ Y ❏ N
_____	_____	❏ Y ❏ N
_____	_____	❏ Y ❏ N
_____	_____	❏ Y ❏ N
_____	_____	❏ Y ❏ N
_____	_____	❏ Y ❏ N
_____	_____	❏ Y ❏ N
_____	_____	❏ Y ❏ N
_____	_____	❏ Y ❏ N
_____	_____	❏ Y ❏ N
_____	_____	❏ Y ❏ N
_____	_____	❏ Y ❏ N

DEGREE_____

Date	Location	Worked?
_____	_____	❏ Y ❏ N
_____	_____	❏ Y ❏ N
_____	_____	❏ Y ❏ N
_____	_____	❏ Y ❏ N
_____	_____	❏ Y ❏ N
_____	_____	❏ Y ❏ N
_____	_____	❏ Y ❏ N
_____	_____	❏ Y ❏ N
_____	_____	❏ Y ❏ N
_____	_____	❏ Y ❏ N
_____	_____	❏ Y ❏ N
_____	_____	❏ Y ❏ N
_____	_____	❏ Y ❏ N
_____	_____	❏ Y ❏ N
_____	_____	❏ Y ❏ N
_____	_____	❏ Y ❏ N
_____	_____	❏ Y ❏ N
_____	_____	❏ Y ❏ N

9 CHARITY WORK/CONTRIBUTIONS

In this section you may list the charity/benevolence work you have performed and/or assisted with and/or contributed to.

WORK

Date	Charity Event/Location	Amount

WORK _____

Date	Charity Event/Location	Amount
_____	_____ __	_____
_____	_____ __	_____
_____	_____ __	_____
_____	_____ __	_____
_____	_____	
_____	_____ __	_____
_____	_____ __	_____
_____	_____ __	_____
_____	_____ __	_____
_____	_____ __	_____
_____	_____ __	_____
_____	_____ __	_____
_____	_____ __	_____
_____	_____ __	_____
_____	_____ __	_____
_____	_____ __	_____

WORK_____

Date	Charity Event/Location	Amount
_____	_____	_____
_____	_____	_____
_____	_____	_____
_____	_____	_____
_____	_____	_____
_____	_____	_____
_____	_____	_____
_____	_____	_____
_____	_____	_____
_____	_____	_____
_____	_____	_____
_____	_____	_____
_____	_____	_____
_____	_____	_____
_____	_____	_____

WORK_____

Date	Charity Event/Location	Amount
_____	_____	_____
_____	_____	_____
_____	_____	_____
_____	_____	_____
_____	_____	_____
_____	_____	_____
_____	_____	_____
_____	_____	_____
_____	_____	_____
_____	_____	_____
_____	_____	_____
_____	_____	_____
_____	_____	_____
_____	_____	_____
_____	_____	_____
_____	_____	_____

WORK

Date	Charity Event/Location	Amount

WORK_____

Date	Charity Event/Location	Amount
_____	_____ __	_____
_____	_____ __	_____
_____	_____ __	_____
_____	_____ __	_____
_____	_____	
_____	_____ __	_____
_____	_____ __	_____
_____	_____ __	_____
_____	_____ __	_____
_____	_____ __	_____
_____	_____ __	_____
_____	_____ __	_____
_____	_____ __	_____
_____	_____ __	_____
_____	_____ __	_____
_____	_____ __	_____

WORK_____

Date	Charity Event/Location	Amount

WORK_____

Date	Charity Event/Location	Amount
_____	_____	_____
_____	_____	_____
_____	_____	_____
_____	_____	_____
_____	_____	_____
_____	_____	_____
_____	_____	_____
_____	_____	_____
_____	_____	_____
_____	_____	_____
_____	_____	_____
_____	_____	_____
_____	_____	_____
_____	_____	_____
_____	_____	_____
_____	_____	_____
_____	_____	_____

WORK

Date	Charity Event/Location	Amount

WORK

Date	Charity Event/Location	Amount
_____	_____ __	_____
_____	_____ __	_____
_____	_____ __	_____
_____	_____ __	_____
_____	_____ __	_____
_____	_____ __	_____
_____	_____ __	_____
_____	_____ __	_____
_____	_____ __	_____
_____	_____ __	_____
_____	_____ __	_____
_____	_____ __	_____
_____	_____ __	_____
_____	_____ __	_____
_____	_____ __	_____
_____	_____ __	_____
_____	_____ __	_____

WORK_____

Date	Charity Event/Location	Amount
_____	_____ __	_____
_____	_____ __	_____
_____	_____ __	_____
_____	_____ __	_____
_____	_____ __	_____
_____	_____ __	_____
_____	_____ __	_____
_____	_____ __	_____
_____	_____ __	_____
_____	_____ __	_____
_____	_____ __	_____
_____	_____ __	_____
_____	_____ __	_____
_____	_____ __	_____
_____	_____ __	_____
_____	_____ __	_____

WORK

Date	Charity Event/Location	Amount

WORK_____

Date	Charity Event/Location	Amount
_____	_____ __	_____
_____	_____ __	_____
_____	_____ __	_____
_____	_____ __	_____
_____	_____ __	_____
_____	_____ __	_____
_____	_____ __	_____
_____	_____ __	_____
_____	_____ __	_____
_____	_____ __	_____
_____	_____ __	_____
_____	_____ __	_____
_____	_____ __	_____
_____	_____ __	_____
_____	_____ __	_____
_____	_____ __	_____

WORK_____

Date	Charity Event/Location	Amount
_____	_____ __	_____
_____	_____ __	_____
_____	_____ __	_____
_____	_____ __	_____
_____	_____ __	_____
_____	_____ __	_____
_____	_____ __	_____
_____	_____ __	_____
_____	_____ __	_____
_____	_____ __	_____
_____	_____ __	_____
_____	_____ __	_____
_____	_____ __	_____
_____	_____ __	_____
_____	_____ __	_____
_____	_____ __	_____

WORK_____

Date	Charity Event/Location	Amount

WORK_____

Date	Charity Event/Location	Amount

WORK_____

Date	Charity Event/Location	Amount
_____	_____	_____
_____	_____	_____
_____	_____	_____
_____	_____	_____
_____	_____	_____
_____	_____	_____
_____	_____	_____
_____	_____	_____
_____	_____	_____
_____	_____	_____
_____	_____	_____
_____	_____	_____
_____	_____	_____
_____	_____	_____
_____	_____	_____
_____	_____	_____

WORK

Date	Charity Event/Location	Amount

WORK

Date	Charity Event/Location	Amount
_____	_____ _	_____
_____	_____ _	_____
_____	_____ _	_____
_____	_____ _	_____
_____	_____ _	_____
_____	_____ _	_____
_____	_____ _	_____
_____	_____ _	_____
_____	_____ _	_____
_____	_____ _	_____
_____	_____ _	_____
_____	_____ _	_____
_____	_____ _	_____
_____	_____ _	_____
_____	_____ _	_____
_____	_____ _	_____
_____	_____ _	_____

10 MASONIC EDUCATION/TRAINING

In this section you may list any Masonic Education trainings, Schools of Instruction, and/or conferences you have participated in, assisted with, or contributed to.

BODY_____

Date	Training Event/Location	
_____	_____	_____
_____	_____	_____
_____	_____	_____
_____	_____	_____
_____	_____	_____
_____	_____	_____
_____	_____	_____
_____	_____	_____
_____	_____	_____
_____	_____	_____
_____	_____	_____
_____	_____	_____
_____	_____	_____
_____	_____	_____
_____	_____	_____
_____	_____	_____

BODY____

Date	Training Event/Location	

BODY_____

Date	Training Event/Location	
_____	_____	_____
_____	_____	_____
_____	_____	_____
_____	_____	_____
_____	_____	_____
_____	_____	_____
_____	_____	_____
_____	_____	_____
_____	_____	_____
_____	_____	_____
_____	_____	_____
_____	_____	_____
_____	_____	_____
_____	_____	_____
_____	_____	_____

BODY_____

Date	Training Event/Location	
_____	_____	_____
_____	_____	_____
_____	_____	_____
_____	_____	_____
_____	_____	_____
_____	_____	_____
_____	_____	_____
_____	_____	_____
_____	_____	_____
_____	_____	_____
_____	_____	_____
_____	_____	_____
_____	_____	_____
_____	_____	_____
_____	_____	_____
_____	_____	_____

BODY___

Date	Training Event/Location	

BODY

Date	Training Event/Location	

BODY_____

Date	Training Event/Location	
_____	_____	_____
_____	_____	_____
_____	_____	_____
_____	_____	_____
_____	_____	_____
_____	_____	_____
_____	_____	_____
_____	_____	_____
_____	_____	_____
_____	_____	_____
_____	_____	_____
_____	_____	_____
_____	_____	_____
_____	_____	_____
_____	_____	_____
_____	_____	_____

BODY___

Date	Training Event/Location	
___	___	___
___	___	___
___	___	___
___	___	___
___	___	___
___	___	___
___	___	___
___	___	___
___	___	___
___	___	___
___	___	___
___	___	___
___	___	___
___	___	___
___	___	___
___	___	___
___	___	___

BODY_____

Date	Training Event/Location	
_____	_____	_____
_____	_____	_____
_____	_____	_____
_____	_____	_____
_____	_____	_____
_____	_____	_____
_____	_____	_____
_____	_____	_____
_____	_____	_____
_____	_____	_____
_____	_____	_____
_____	_____	_____
_____	_____	_____
_____	_____	_____
_____	_____	_____
_____	_____	_____
_____	_____	_____

BODY_____

Date	Training Event/Location
_____	_____ _____
_____	_____ _____
_____	_____ _____
_____	_____ _____
_____	_____ _____
_____	_____ _____
_____	_____ _____
_____	_____ _____
_____	_____ _____
_____	_____ _____
_____	_____ _____
_____	_____ _____
_____	_____ _____
_____	_____ _____
_____	_____ _____
_____	_____ _____
_____	_____ _____
_____	_____ _____

BODY_____

Date	Training Event/Location	
_____	_____	_____
_____	_____	_____
_____	_____	_____
_____	_____	_____
_____	_____	_____
_____	_____	_____
_____	_____	_____
_____	_____	_____
_____	_____	_____
_____	_____	_____
_____	_____	_____
_____	_____	_____
_____	_____	_____
_____	_____	_____
_____	_____	_____

BODY___

Date	Training Event/Location	

BODY_____

Date	Training Event/Location	
_____	_____	_____
_____	_____	_____
_____	_____	_____
_____	_____	_____
_____	_____	_____
_____	_____	_____
_____	_____	_____
_____	_____	_____
_____	_____	_____
_____	_____	_____
_____	_____	_____
_____	_____	_____
_____	_____	_____
_____	_____	_____
_____	_____	_____

BODY_____

Date	Training Event/Location	

BODY_____

Date	Training Event/Location	
_____	_____	_____
_____	_____	_____
_____	_____	_____
_____	_____	_____
_____	_____	_____
_____	_____	_____
_____	_____	_____
_____	_____	_____
_____	_____	_____
_____	_____	_____
_____	_____	_____
_____	_____	_____
_____	_____	_____
_____	_____	_____
_____	_____	_____
_____	_____	_____

BODY_____

Date	Training Event/Location	
_____	_____	_____
_____	_____	_____
_____	_____	_____
_____	_____	_____
_____	_____	_____
_____	_____	_____
_____	_____	_____
_____	_____	_____
_____	_____	_____
_____	_____	_____
_____	_____	_____
_____	_____	_____
_____	_____	_____
_____	_____	_____
_____	_____	_____
_____	_____	_____
_____	_____	_____

BODY_____

Date	Training Event/Location	
_____	_____	_____
_____	_____	_____
_____	_____	_____
_____	_____	_____
_____	_____	_____
_____	_____	_____
_____	_____	_____
_____	_____	_____
_____	_____	_____
_____	_____	_____
_____	_____	_____
_____	_____	_____
_____	_____	_____
_____	_____	_____
_____	_____	_____
_____	_____	_____

BODY_____

Date	Training Event/Location	
_____	_____	____
_____	_____	____
_____	_____	____
_____	_____	____
_____	_____	____
_____	_____	____
_____	_____	____
_____	_____	____
_____	_____	____
_____	_____	____
_____	_____	____
_____	_____	____
_____	_____	____
_____	_____	____
_____	_____	____
_____	_____	____

BODY_____

Date   Training Event/Location

_____   _____   _____

_____   _____   _____

_____   _____   _____

_____   _____   _____

_____   _____   _____

_____   _____   _____

_____   _____   _____

_____   _____   _____

_____   _____   _____

_____   _____   _____

_____   _____   _____

_____   _____   _____

_____   _____   _____

_____   _____   _____

_____   _____   _____

_____   _____   _____

Notes

Notes

Notes

Notes

Notes

Notes

Notes

Notes

Notes

Notes

ABOUT THE AUTHOR

The Author, James F. "Chip" Hatcher III, is a Freemason and member of several regular, concordant, appendant, associated, allied, and invitational Masonic Bodies.

He lives in the foothills of the Great Smoky Mountains in Eastern Tennessee with his wife Lisa, 3 children, 3 cats, and regularly encourages other to continually seek more light through the pathways of Freemasonry.

OTHER MASONIC BOOKS
BY THE AUTHOR

at

masonicpress.com

Worshipful Master's Guidebook

The Lodge Officer's Handbook

King Solomon's Passport

Masonic Roll of Fellow Crafts

Mark Masters Lodge Book of Marks

York Rite Mason's Handbook

Scottish Rite Mason's Handbook

SO•MOTE•IT•BE

Made in the USA
Coppell, TX
21 September 2024

37535753R00103